SOOOOP
SPIDERS

By Gerry McCarton

Illustrated by Karen Sayles

McCarton Books

Published by McCarton
Deals Cottage
6 Cragg View
Pool in Wharfedale
Leeds
LS21 1DW

gerry1_mccarton@yahoo.co.uk

Printed by Shipley Print Co Ltd. Bradford
01274 530041.

For my gorgeous grandchildren, Joshua and Cayleigh and my Godson Kieran Smith, as I promised. I would like to thank my wife, Maggie who without a whinge listened to my story several times from beginning to end. My two boys, Aaron and Keir, who gently advised me many years ago,

"Dad, you can't write"

And not forgetting my patient, amazing typist, Kath Sinclair, who managed to decipher my hand written notes.

Gerry McCarton has also written "The House With No Snow" 2006

Sooooperb Spiders

Contents

Chapter 1 The Storm

Chapter 2 The Dangerous Jungle

Chapter 3 The Gentle Creatures

Chapter 4 The Humming Cloud

Chapter 5 Sally and Sam Surrender

Chapter 6 Ice Prison

Chapter 7 The Humans

CHAPTER 1

THE STORM

The sky was dark, rain clouds blocked off the sun, turning day to night. It had rained for days; the Spider family's home in the corner of the garden had been completely destroyed by huge drops of rain.

Everywhere insects were dashing around frantic to find shelter from the storm. Some carried children on their backs, while others struggled with food and luggage. The hazards of crossing huge streams formed by the continuous rain took their toll. Puddles had

come to resemble large lakes or seas with waves crashing all around. Some insects were carried away by the movement of the water. Drowned, never to be seen again by parents and family.

Sally spider had been standing on a large stone, watching the rain bounce down all around her. A large number of raindrops hit her so hard they knocked her off her perch and into the river of rain. The flow of the water carried her quickly down the footpath and in the direction of the house gully, which took all the water to the smelly drains below and certain death.

"Dad! Dad! I can't swim!" shouted Sally.

"Swim Sally, kick your legs" shouted her Mum.

"This is your fault!" cried Mr Spider. "You should have taken her to swimming lessons!"

"My fault! Why am I to blame? I take the kids everywhere, I do everything" said Mrs Spider. "You don't catch flies or anything. I bring all the food home; I'm fed up sitting round the web patiently waiting, while you…"

"Shut up you two!" shouted their son Sam, "Our Sally is drowning! Quick, quick do something!"

"Kick your legs Sally!" urged Mr and Mrs Spider. "Kick them hard, you've got to swim!"

Slowly but surely, Sally got closer and closer to the shore, until at last her parents were able to pull her out. Gasping, exhausted, but safe, Sally was dried off by her Dad and Mum.

"We would have been better staying home Dad!" shivered a frozen Sally.

"We can't stay there Sally, our home is destroyed every year, you know that. The house will be safer and warmer for us, and it's today or never, I suppose" said Mr Spider. "There will be no more children hitting us with balls, no more cats and dogs crashing into our home. We will never get wet again or freeze when it snows. In the house we will only have to worry about humans and then only look for food when it gets dark."

The spider family had been thinking for months about moving into the house that shared their garden. But Mum and Dad had always said no, it was too dangerous to mix with people.

"Come on then!" said Mr Spider to Sally and Sam, "people do not like us spiders so if you see one, freeze or hide quickly because if they spot you, you will be crushed."

"Why don't they like us Mum?" Sally asked.

"Oh, I don't know" sighed Sally's Mum, "It has always been like that even when Mum and Gran were little so I suppose it'll always be the case. People just don't like us spiders. I think they are frightened of the way we look. Some humans are always frightened of something that's different to them."

"The way we look!" shrieked Sally angrily. "We look OK, we dress OK. Great in fact, and smell sooooperb, we are so clean. There won't be many insects as clean as we are Mum! I mean we don't go eating people's food like flies do, making them sick and ill and we do not sting people like bees or wasps do, or act like some animals who bite people. I just can't understand it," said Sally. "We catch and eat all their flies, and what do they do in return? They chase and hurt us. What's wrong with human beings, can't they see we are good to have around their house, we're much better than bleach and disinfectant. They stink! We are so cool. Human beings are so shady and so stupid.
By now, with all the talking they had reached the house, and ran in under the door.

"Stop!" shouted Dad. "Stay here until I come back, I have lived with people before, I know how to avoid being caught."

"Sam , look after Mum and Sally, you're older and the man when I am not around." Sally, looking annoyed, screamed at her dad,

"I don't! We don't need Sam to look after us; we can look after ourselves, thank you Dad."

Dad had been gone for ages, Sam thought the worst.

.

"I have a feeling Dad's been caught. Where will he be Mum, will he be a prisoner, locked up in chains?" murmured Sally.

"No dear, I don't think so, your Dad will be alright, he knows how to avoid people."

Peeping out from underneath the shadow of the large kitchen door, the children could see a bright light hanging from the ceiling. Alongside one wall and fixed to it was a radiator with the family cat asleep in front, not knowing the spiders were moving into the house. Shivering with cold but feeling warmer by the minute, the children watched the kitchen floor for signs of their Dad. Finally he appeared, breathless, but OK.

"Come on everyone, quickly while the house cat is asleep and the people are out. We can find somewhere safe to live without being seen."

The family who were living behind the bookshelf had hardly been in the house a day, when Sally and Sam heard voices coming from the hallway. With mum and dad out hunting for food, the pair decided to investigate. Dropping down to the floor, they ran through the open door into the hall. There, playing football, were three spider children from next door. The children, who were a little older than Sally and Sam, invited them to join in the fun.

After a while the children heard a loud bang as the front door was slammed shut. The walls shuddered and the floor shook so hard dust and children were sent sky wards, bouncing them high into the air, as a shadow covered the whole floor,

'HUMANS" Shouted the other children, as they all scattered to avoid being killed or hurt. Sally, thinking quickly, grabbed Sam by his hair and pulled him under a newspaper, that had been delivered through the letter box .

They heard a scream for help then a loud thud. Sally peeped out from under the newspaper to see a human foot stamp down hard on top of their new friends.

"Quick Sam, while there's no one looking, we have to escape the giant foot."

Running alongside the skirting board, they bumped into Mum and Dad returning home with no food. Mum and Dad had seen the danger.
"You two! We told you to stay home, hidden. See what happens when you don't do as you're told."

"Those poor children, let's get you home where it's safe."

Once they arrived home, Mum and Dad said there wasn't any food available and so everyone should try to get some sleep. After some time everyone went to sleep, except of course Sally. She had pretended to be asleep, opening one eye. She quickly woke Sam. "Come on let's go for a walk and explore, Mum and Dad will be asleep for days."

Out through the lounge and into the hallway ran the excited brother and sister in search of food and fun.

"A tasty fly burger would suit me just fine," said Sam.

"One fly burger, don't you mean two or three? I am absolutely starving," said a hungry Sally.

"Thinking about food, don't you think a lightly cooked wasp on toast would be nicer?" said Sally, "mmmmm", with saliva running down her chin.

"Followed by a long juicy drink of dung beetle sweat, I can taste it now" said Sam, sticking his tongue out and licking the sweet liquid that was running down his face, over his eyes and nose. In fact it was everywhere. "Delicious" said a satisfied Sam. But it was not what Sam thought it was, it was drops of water that were showering down on them high above from the mouth of the house cat. She had woken up and was directly behind them. Clawing the air and spitting her saliva everywhere. Sally grabbed Sam and dragged him into a crack in the wall, just before the cat's paw flew through the air, damaging and scratching the wallpaper.

"That was lucky," said a breathless Sally trying to stay calm, "now where are we? "

CHAPTER 2

THE DANGEROUS JUNGLE

It was dusty and dark inside the wall, Sam hung on tight to Sally.

"Sally! I want to go home, "cried Sam.   "Well Sam, if we go out there we will be eaten alive, we might as well stay here and look for food" whispered a frightened Sally, trying to sound tough.

Working their way along a narrow ledge, they passed an old earwig suicidally sucking in the fumes of another cigarette. Sally and Sam had never seen anything like it. A rumble caused them to look around, the bus had arrived. It was battered like it had been on an African Safari. How little did they know?

'All aboard" shouted a voice.

Sally and Sam sat down ready for the unknown journey. It was a long ride and they had both fallen asleep when the bus jerked to a stop and woke them up.

'I wonder where we are?" said a tired Sam.

'Probably somewhere inside the house wall!" said Sally.

'Inside" said the old earwig who had been listening to everything. 'We are not inside your house, we are underground now, didn't you know this bus brought insects to the weekly market?"

"Wow," shouted Sam, "look at that sight."

It was a valley about one hundred metres below them, it looked like an African plain. Springs, rivers and swamps.

"That valley is dangerous," warned the earwig. "Stay here, if you want to go back, the earthworm will take you." spluttered the fag waving insect, as he wandered off.

"Come on Sam, we're going down for a cool drink and a bath and maybe some food" sighed Sally.

"Just think of all those midges, mmmmmm bet I can get five in my gob all at once" laughed Sam.
It didn't take them long to reach the valley. Sam was shivering with fear. Sally noticed and hugged him close.

"See Sam, there's nothing to fear."

Walking down a path they found a cool stream; Sally and Sam gulped the refreshing water down and began to clean their teeth and toenails.
Sally laid back to do some sunbathing and fell asleep while Sam carefully cut his nails on a sharp rock sticking out of the water. The tree above Sam was losing its leaves. Sam watched for a second or two, they looked pretty as they fell to earth spiralling down like a helicopter. This is perfect thought Sam. That is until the earwig arrived. He spoke so softly, Sam had to almost shove his head into the earwig's mouth to hear what was being said.

'Quick kids while there is time, over here."

Sam spun around looking confused. "What are you talking about?"

"Shush," butted in the earwig, "no time to talk, just take a look at those leaves, they are changing shape as they hit the ground."

Without making it obvious, Sam squinted out of the corner of his eye; sure enough the earwig was right. The leaves were changing shape, from being flat to looking like a jellyfish and were heading in Sally and Sam's direction. Sally was still asleep, Sam gave her a nudge.

"Sally, psst, Sally, psst wake up quick."

Sally yawned and stretched.

"What's up Sam, why are you shouting in my ear hole?"

Sam blurted out, "The leaves on the trees are falling and..."

Sally cut in "Yes, I know Sam, leaves on trees do fall to the ground, it's called gravity."

"Yes, but not in the summer time, they don't." shouted a terrified

Sam, who continued to watch them change shape.

Sally sat upright and, taking a peek through her half-closed eyes, saw them herself. Slipping and sliding along the ground like ice skaters, but without their boots. The earwig spotted the danger and grabbing the pair, dragged them off.

"In here," shouted the earwig.

It was a hole barely big enough for the earwig to squeeze into, but Sally and Sam somehow managed to make it, crawling along behind the earwig. Every step was harder and harder. The hole had now become a tunnel, and this too was getting smaller and narrower. They continued until a wall of soil stood in their way. With their backs to the wall the trio clung to each other in terror, not knowing what to do, what to expect from the quivering, slimy jelly.

Eventually, the earwig broke the silence. "I, er, think we are safe here kids, they, whatever they are, are too big and fat to get down here. We will just have to sit tight until they get fed up of waiting and go."

Sally interrupted. "Why are they chasing us Earwig? We are only kids, we can't hurt them."

"Yes, I know you are," said the earwig, "but they are frightened of you, you see I crept up into the tree, they didn't spot me, I am so small. They are frightened of how you look, I am sorry, they are not used to seeing spiders."

Sally could not hold back her temper. "What! What's wrong with everything, why doesn't anything we meet like us? If it isn't humans, it's insects, cats, dogs and now these things I can't understand it, we're not that bad. I would like to know what is ugly, what does it mean and what is normal?"

"Well," said the earwig, "you are not ugly, it is just that anything which looks different to the majority is picked on and called names. We earwigs get chased and killed as well, but have more legs than you and escape quicker." Earwig knew he had to change the subject to calm them both down. "I suggest we have a sing-song, so who is going to start?"

"I will," said Sally, "I like the one about spiders. My Mum used to sing it to me when I was little", so she began:

> "Humans love us do
> No flies in your stew
> No spit on your sandwiches
> Or no running to the loo
> We keep your home free of flies, wasps and bees
> A friend we aim to please
> So be aware and be fair when you see a spider."

"Lovely Sally, lovely, now I've got one." said the earwig, trying to keep the momentum going in order to keep their minds off the jellies.

"Do the jellies wriggle and waggle, quiver and quarrel, bicker and baggle,
I never know which end to ogle.
My mind boggles do we chew 'em, or boot 'em like a ball
Or throw them like a snowball and splat them on the wall.
Do we..."

"Ssh, Earwig" whispered Sally, "can you hear anything?"

They sat silent as mice, the only sound coming from the beat of their hearts.

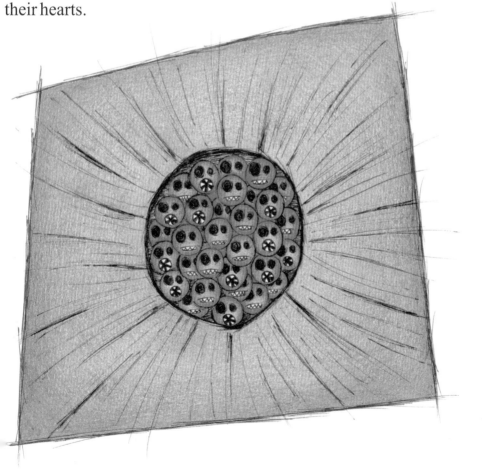

"Can't you hear it Earwig?" urged Sally.

"I'm not sure, what is it you can hear?"

"A sort of scraping noise," whispered Sally.

Through the inky darkness they spotted something moving towards them.

"It's only a worm." said Sam.

But it wasn't, it was the jellies. They had changed shape, and now looked like cooked spaghetti, not mashed together, but like an army of soldiers. Bending and twisting their way through the tunnel, twenty-five abreast.

CHAPTER 3

THE GENTLE CREATURES

The trio's path was blocked by a wall of soil. They were trapped, and in the darkness and distance of the tunnel, they could hear, the voices of the jellies fast approaching.

It became obvious the jellies were coming for Sally and Sam and, with a wall of soil at their backs, they would soon be found and captured.

Fumbling around in the darkness, a frightened Sally whispered to Earwig "Do something Earwig, you're the grown up".

"Earwig! Earwig! Where are you?" she whispered.

"Sam! Is Earwig with you?"

"No Sally. He's with you" whispered Sam.

As Sam said this, something brushed past him, almost knocking him over into Sally's arms. It was a giant earthworm.

'Look you two, Earwig has disappeared. You had better follow me, they will be here any second. I will take you to a place of safety. They're out to kill you."

Sally and Sam quickly grabbed the giant Earthworm as it burrowed into the wall of soil, dragging Sally and Sam behind it. As it moved forwards soil fell into place to hide their escape.

Eventually the tunnel opened up into a clearing, with a valley on one side, and tunnels going in every direction; almost like a large roundabout where roads take people to different places like towns and cities.

"You'll be safe here. I'm not heading for the human world today. I have got to visit family. But any earthworm will take you up if you stand by that large bush. You will only have to wait a few hours at the most," and off he went.

Sally and Sam sat down and waited and waited. Hours passed. Evening was fast approaching and with it frost. They sheltered under the leaves of the bush, whose branches trailed along the carpet of the clearing.

They woke surrounded by strange looking creatures. One had the facial features of a human. Another the eyes and nose of a bee, while his arms and legs were that of a human. Another had the ears of a fox, face of a human and body of a gorilla, and so on.

The gorilla approached Sally, half walking, half crawling. The creature attempted to stand up, but was too weak and stumbled forward, unable to walk. Seeing that the creature was in distress, Sally got up and went to the spot where the creature had fallen.

"I am Clarbo," he groaned. His eyes were bloodshot, and his lips were sore, swollen and cracked. His tongue was blue, almost black. He explained he had been the local doctor but was no longer.

"The population is dying. Not many of us left," he murmured. He explained that their source of water had dried up and was controlled by an evil race of jellyflies.

"They use water to punish us and any other creature that disagrees with them," he moaned. "Look across the valley." He pointed to a mountainside, about a mile away. It was covered in lush vegetation with a gorgeous colourful meadow below.

"All the water is stored across there in huge dams. We used to go to the valley for water but now if we went we would be captured and possibly killed."

Sally could see that with the sun constantly shining and no water to drink, these creatures were drying out. Even though this was not a desert, these creatures were suffering as if it was. Only plants were surviving with their roots digging deep into the soil for sources of water.

Friendships were quickly made.

"So where are you from?" one of them shouted.

"We have never seen anything as beautiful as you two."

And Sally had never heard anything as beautiful as those words. "Me! Us beautiful!" she thought. "We are from the human world," shouted Sally.

The crowd were hushed by a child crying. It was Sam.

"What is wrong little one?" said a voice from the crowd.

"I am hungry and want my Mum!" cried Sam.

"Oh it is my little bro, I promised I would find him some food. That was ages ago. We are really starving. We haven't eaten in weeks," said Sally.

"We have lots of food," the crowd chorused.

Sally and Sam were shown a variety of different vegetarian foods. There were leaves of all colours, shapes and sizes. There was a yellow leaf that resembled butter on the outside and tasted of vanilla ice cream in the middle. One leaf resembled a strawberry on one side and blueberry on the other, while its stem tasted of rhubarb and custard. Some were chocolate brown "And yes it does indeed taste of creamy chocolate," said a voice.

'I am sorry," said Sally "but we don't eat vegetables."

'But that is all we have, we stopped eating meat years ago," they said.

'Mmm let me explain, said a frustrated and hungry Sally. "We spiders eat live food, for example, a nice fat caterpillar would suit me just fine, or even a rotting old wasp would do."

'Emmm, sounds so good Sally, I am so hungry," moaned Sam.

A silence fell around the crowd. "How cruel," muttered a moth.

'How gross, disgusting," screamed a mother caterpillar, stooping to pick up her youngsters, before disappearing into bushes.

Sally quickly realised her mistake and that she was talking to creatures and insects she would normally eat. Spotting there were no flies in the crowd, which were the main diet of spiders, she decided to stand her ground and hope for the best.

'Can't you lot take a joke? It was just a joke, after all it's a well known fact that spiders only ever eat flies …"

"Flies! Flies! Is that another joke? You are of course joking. You must be joking. Please tell us you are," urged voices from the crowd.

"Na. We don't joke about food, not when we're starving. Flies, yes we love them. Why, don't you? Mmmmm so juicy," slurped Sally.

The noise among the creatures and insects was deafening, until a female voice exploded above the chatter of the crowd, which opened showing a path that led to a beautiful female butterfly sitting on a rose petal. That is to say, she was a butterfly from her wings to her body but had the face of a human.

She explained to Sally and Sam there was an evil race of creatures called the jellyflies. Nothing escaped from them. She pointed out that some creatures were tortured, while others were eaten alive.

"They have even toasted our friends and family, the butterflies, and used them as crisps, or sold them to other creatures as food. So cruel. You are better turning round and going home. Flies are so dangerous. No one can stop them," she said.

"No! No!" some shouted, "We need you to help us. We are now too weak to search for water."

"There is water directly below us. Come look." They showed Sally an opening in the ground, similar to a crack in the pavement.

"It is very deep but there is water down there. We are just too large to fit down but you two are so small you could just save us. If we give you the roots of this friendly plant it will reach into the water below and suck up water to save us," pleaded their desperate, gentle new friends.

Sally felt she had to try to help them, before taking the advice of the beautiful butterfly and head home.

"Evil flies or not, we will do it. Come on Sam!" said Sally.

"I just cannot believe these evil creatures are flies but if that is the case, our Sam and me will have a few Flyburgers when down there," joked Sally.

"Stop!" shouted another voice. It was the giant earthworm. "Those things that were chasing you are not just flies as you known them in the human world, they are super flies. They breathe ice and change shape whenever they need to," exclaimed the worm.

"But that can't be true," said a bewildered Sally. "What we saw were leaves falling out of a tree and somehow they skated along the ground like jelly."

"No they did not fall, they flew, so as not to alarm you. They changed shape to look like leaves off a tree," murmured the earthworm.

"Of course, it all makes sense now. I remember thinking leaves don't fall from trees in the spring time," said Sally.

"Ah, so you are agreeing then. It is the jellyflies who keep us all here trapped! They cannot get in, we cannot get out," grumbled the crowd. "We too change shape almost daily. That way we will spot an intruder. We will never leave here, only the earthworms come and go, filling in the tunnels as they go. This is our sanctuary."

"Ok," said an impatient Sally, "let's drop down into this hole Sam and find water for this gentle crowd."

"Please do not go down there," said an older insect. "You do not have to go down that dark, deep hole alone. You, like us, don't know what is down there. You could get trapped and we wouldn't be able to help you. You can still find the water to help us by going down that mountain track. That way you will not be ambushed as easily. But be warned, no one ever returns from there," said the frail insect.

"We will take care," said Sally as she grabbed Sam's hand and started to walk towards the mountain track.

A voice boomed out again. "It is us who should be going for water not these children." It was the beautiful butterfly.

That said the pair set off on the long walk across the mountain top

CHAPTER 4

THE HUMMING CLOUD

The path was indeed dangerous but the danger was not from the predatory flies, but swampy ground that threatened to suck them down. The boulders were like mountains to them, any trip could result in a broken leg.

Hour after hour they climbed and clambered under a sweltering sun. Gasping for water and weak from lack of food, the pair decided to rest. It was at this point they heard a low humming sound, the sort of noise we hear when a bee floats around the room, or a helicopter passes overhead.

Looking up at the sky, they spotted a large cloud in the distance. The most enormous cloud formation they had ever seen and slowly it began to block out the sun, until all around became darker. As this was happening the air around them began to get wild, like a hurricane was about to hit them. Hanging on tight to a branch of a bush they suddenly began to realise the danger they were in.

It was not a cloud heading in their direction but hundreds, thousands of jellyflies, and the beat of their wings was creating a mini hurricane. The jellyflies were soon upon the mesmerised brother and sister. Sally, realising this, said to Sam, "That's not a cloud Sam. I mean it is thousands, maybe millions of flies. We have to get off this mountain top and into that valley pretty quick. When I say jump, jump."

"But it's too high Sally, we might get hurt. Can't we use our silk web and catch a few of them?"

"Sam! Can't you see what I can see, there are thousands of them. We won't have any time to use our silk, so we have to jump. It's straight down on our bums."

Looking around she saw a large oak leaf and grabbed it. "When I say go, go Sam."

"But we might get hurt Sally. Why don't we stop and talk to them."

"Ye! We will die if we stay here stupid! They want to eat us silly!" Sally grabbed hold of Sam and jumped off the cliff top.

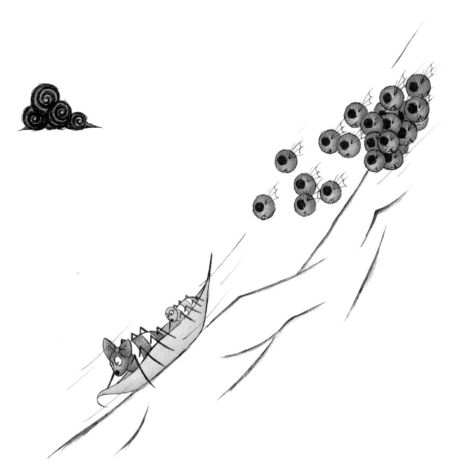

As they slid down the mountain side, Sally glanced behind her. The ﬂies had changed course. They were now following; chasing Sally and Sam!

"See that grassy field Sam. We need to get to it quickly and hide if we can."

Sliding and tumbling down the mountain side the pair could feel the air and ground getting colder. The jellyflies were spraying a liquid into the air that fell on the ground, turning it into a glacier.

Though the pair were moving quicker now on ice, just like a sledge they were also freezing cold. The flies were catching up fast and just as they prepared to strike, a gust of wind appeared.

It first blew the jellyflies backwards almost to the top of the mountain. Then returning almost as quickly to lift Sally and Sam up onto the air, a glove like feeling surrounded them as the children were lifted skywards. As Sally and Sam hung on tight to the leaf watching the earth disappear below, a gentle voice was heard.

"I am the power of the wind. I rescued you from the jellyflies because you are the first ones to leave the prison of dryness to seek out water. Be careful though, the jellyflies know you are here. They will come looking for you," he said as he placed them gently on the ground.

As this was said the wind disappeared as quickly as it had arrived.

"Did that really happen Sam? It's so strange here, at least those flies did not catch us," said Sally.

As Sally said this the sky again grew dark. They had not realised with talking, the jellyflies were almost upon them. Millions of them blocked out the sun's rays. Darkness covered the earth.

"It is the jellyflies Sam. Run to that field of grass just there." The pair ran for their lives, reaching the grass as the air around them became chilled once more and the ground began to freeze. The children began to panic.

"There is no where to run Sam. No hiding place," cried Sally. Getting as deep into the field as they could, the pair stopped to catch their breath, but only momentarily. They soon began to feel chilled again as the jellyflies got closer, hovering just above the grass. Inspecting each blade as they went. Looking up, Sally and Sam could almost see the colour of their bellies. The brother and sister began to shiver and, as they hugged to stay warm, Sally whispered to Sam to cheer him up. "One or two jellyflies Sam, or maybe half a dozen, but we have no chance with this lot bro ..."

Just then, Sally felt a shudder on the ground, again and again. The earth all around was moving. Sally recognised what was happening. It was the jellyflies again. They had changed shape and were starting to march through the grass in their thousands in the shape of spaghetti. She remembered the tunnel just before the earthworm saved them. Orders were now being shouted by the jellyfly in charge.

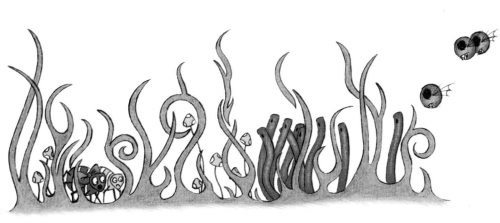

"We want them alive. We must find out who they are and how they got here. We do not want more like them in our world."

"I am sorry Sam, this really does look like the end. I am so cold, brrrr, freezing." As she said this the grass all around appeared to come alive. Blades of grass opened up. This amazed Sally who stood wide eyed, unable to believe what she was seeing or hearing.

"Look, you two. You will freeze out there. Climb inside, you will be warmer and safer," said the grass.

"What if it wants to swallow us Sally?" cried Sam.

"We have no choice Sam, let's get inside."

Sally and Sam quickly climbed inside a blade of grass as it closed itself, just seconds before the jellyflies arrived.

They were in their thousands, twisting and turning, inspecting each blade as they trampled through the field of grass, looking for Sally and Sam. Meanwhile the pair remained safe and warm as the army of flies disappeared, and the sound of marching had stopped.

A day had passed. Sally and Sam had just said their goodbyes and were ready to leave and go back to the human world when a message was given to them by the older blades of grass.

"The flies have not gone but are waiting, surrounding the field in their millions, waiting for you to come out. They are determined to get you. Stay here children, do not go out. They will kill you. We can keep you hidden and safe," said the older grasses.

"They will get fed up and go. You'll see!" Twenty four hours had passed with the flies constantly hovering overhead. The noise of their wings had made it impossible for either Sally and Sam, or the grasses to get sleep. By the third day a message was received.

"If you do not surrender those children we will set fire to you. "

"They will burn us to the ground!" some said. "I do not want to die like that," went the younger ones.

"We must hand them over, we have never been the enemy of the flies so why start now. These are just strangers who will soon disappear, saving themselves while we will die like the rest who challenge the flies," went the cry.

"Ok! Ok! I, I mean we agree with you. We do not want you hurt in any way," said a concerned Sally.

"No that would be a coward's way and, after all, these are just children, just children," exclaimed the elders.

"But we cannot allow you to suffer for us," said Sally. As she said this, there was the faint smell of smoke. Chaos soon followed. Young and old grasses, on the perimeter of the field began to burn.

There was now no escape. All around them was ablaze. The grasses began to stampede, choking with smoke. Everything was either crushed or dying of smoke inhalation. Suddenly the smoke was dispersed by a gust of wind. At the same time droplets of rain could be felt, until large drops as big as tennis balls were landing and astonishingly began to put out the fire. A stream soon appeared that ran to the river.

The wind that had saved their lives earlier had watched the evil jellyfiies set fire to the grass.

"I had to help you," it said, "the killing has to stop, plus I am pretty lonely most days with everyone I know a prisoner of the flies in some way or other. I used to enjoy carrying insects around the world and doing my job in nature, that is until the flies took over. We must take a stand against them. If we do not I will die of loneliness," whispered the wind.

Sally and Sam looked on bewildered unable to believe what they had just seen and heard and how lucky they were.

"Where are you," said Sam "Why can't we see you?"

"I am all around. I live here in this world and also in the human world but like everything around us I will die too if we do not stop the flies," whispered the gentle wind.

As this was being said, the brother and sister were lifted off the ground and sat on a raft of seaweed that stood in the stream.

"Stay on the raft. It will not sink but will take you to safety. Do not return but do tell the world about the evil flies."

The raft began to move along the fast flowing stream very quickly, passing other creatures intent on saving their own lives. The stream soon joined a river and in the distance Sally could see snow covered mountains.

"Hey Sam, snow!" shouted Sally. "Fancy a snowball fight bro?"

"Ok, yep, anything sounds better than fighting the jellyflies," laughed Sam.

"My Mum and Dad won't believe it, flies in control," giggled Sally.

CHAPTER 5

SALLY AND SAM SURRENDER

The river soon joined a wild sea, a sea of floating ice. Icebergs taller than the trees or buildings in their home town towered over them. This was not the kind of snow or fun Sally had in mind. Her eye caught a floating iceberg passing by. Inside it, and frozen was one of the creatures she had chatted to earlier, completely frozen like a shop window dummy. His mouth and eyes open as though about to speak.

"It must have frozen while sitting on ice like these around us Sam and we will freeze too if we do not get off this raft and onto dry land."

The raft of seaweed drifted along taken by the currents and bouncing into gigantic icebergs. One of these was so big it pushed Sally and Sam onto land, covered in snow and ice.

On to the packed ice Sally and Sam jumped. It was then they both became really frightened. As far as they could see was covered in snow and ice.

"We have to walk Sam. Got to keep warm" said Sally as she pulled her brother to her. They walked for what seemed like hours, with the cold icy wind blowing and blasting them in their faces as they stumbled through a blizzard of snow.

"We must find shelter soon Sam. I am so hungry I could eat a scabby fly or two or three or a juicy caterpillar."

Looking around she realised Sam was not there. He was no where to be seen.

"Sam! Sam! Where are you?" shouted Sally, frantically running back into the blizzard to find Sam. He was fast asleep or nearly fast asleep, laying there on the snowy ground, curled up.

Sally pulled and tugged Sam "Wake up Sam. You can't fall asleep, We have got to keep awake".

As Sam stirred Sally picked him up and held him tight to her body to warm him.

"We can't sleep here Sam, we will die doing that. You have got to help me Sam."

Sam began to wake up and the pair again continued their perilous journey. After what seemed like eternity, Sally spotted a cave in the distance. "That cave will shelter us Sam. We will soon be there," said Sally, as the cold sleet and wind began nipping her feet and nose. The pair were near to death as they reached the cave. Sally knew she had to spin as much silk as possible to wrap around her and Sam to keep out the biting cold.

The cave was dark, high and long. Sally thought it would be safer climbing high and if an intruder came they would be woken by the tug on Sally's silky webbing.
Some warm air occasionally drifted through the canopy of the cave, providing just enough warmth for Sally and Sam to slip into a deep sleep.

They were woken by the sound of running water.
"Water Sam! That is what we came for. Let's go collect it and off home we go bro."

After some time they noticed the air in the cave getting warmer, just enough to beat off the biting frost of the morning. Eventually they left the cave, finding themselves on a cliff path. Down below them the landscape was shrouded in mist and visible at ground level, just below the mist, was a snowy slope which was melting. The melting snow was forming a stream that led to a patch of grass and there, as the sun soaked up the morning mist, thousands of flies were basking and preening themselves in the sun's rays.

"They look so aggressive," said Sam.

"No they don't. I've seen tougher looking gold fish," said Sally, turning to Sam. "If those jellyflies got here there must be a way out, but first we must collect water for our friends."

Crouching behind a large rock Sally and Sam filled two bucket shaped containers given to them by the gentle creatures. With the water collected, Sally pointed to a path in the distance that seemed to climb upwards to the top of the cliff.

"Let's head for that path while they're distracted". Sally and Sam climbed slowly up the steep side of the cliff. Down below them ran the stream and the sleepy flies. Sally's bag carrying the water got caught on a loose rock and it was sent bouncing down the cliff face splashing into the stream below. This alerted three guards who patrolled the area. Immediately they flew towards the cliff looking to investigate the danger.

Sally and Sam sat nervously behind a large boulder watching them get closer and closer. Suddenly she had an idea.

"Sam there're only three of them. Pull your silk out and lasso the one over there. I will get the other two."

It was the only choice Sally had, the jellyflies would have found them and they may never have seen Mum or Dad ever again. Sam's fly approached from a different direction and was a bit behind the other two that Sally had in her sight. Sally acted instinctively, pulling out her silk and shaping it into a lasso. Once her silky lasso hit the first jellyfly it stuck to it like glue. She hauled it in to her and wrapped it up within two seconds. The other fly, seeing there was danger, turned around to warn the others. As he was about to sound the alarm, Sally struck again. The lasso of sticky silk hit it so quickly, it was wrapped up into a ball alongside the other one in seconds.

Sam followed suit and the three guards were quickly disabled, completely wrapped up in sticky webbing. Sally knew it would

not be long before these guards were reported missing and a party would be sent looking for them.

"We have got to climb fast Sam. They will soon come looking for these three goops. As they ran to climb they realised the path was blocked by hundreds of flies.

Sally and Sam were stuck. They could not go back or forward.

A message was delivered to them.

"Surrender immediately. You are trapped. We will wait a short while. If we do not receive a reply by the time the sun leaves the mountain top we will cause a landslide and crush you."

Sally was thinking quickly and looking around frantically for a way out, thinking she could bluff them. "We hold three of your guards. They will die too," shouted Sally.

"Those are only three. We can afford to lose them. We are millions," came the reply.

As this was being said, Sally and Sam heard a voice, a familiar voice. It was the beautiful butterfly. "Hey you two jump on board. I have been looking everywhere for you. These monsters killed my family. I just had to help."

The children saw their chance and jumped. Butterfly flew as quickly as possible extending her wings to the fullest to gain height, and go above the flies. Within minutes they were surrounded by a dozen or more flies that landed on the beautiful butterfly and forced her to land in their fortress below.

Everywhere Sally looked there were insects frozen into slabs of ice. "Look Sam, just like the insects on the sea of ice," whispered Sally.

As she was talking a spray of freezing vapour began to cover the trio. Just enough spray to freeze the skin, a similar feeling to when children and adults have played in

the snow. Sally was unable to defend herself or the others as she helplessly watched the flies breaking off leaves from a nearby bush and then started to wrap the leaves around the trio going from head to toe. This done the brother and sister were dropped into ice cold water up to their necks.

The water began to turn into a block of ice. "It looks like we lost Sam. Look, there is the butterfly ready to be roasted over that fire and there is nothing we can do," murmured Sally. "It may be our turn next bro".

"What Sally. I cannot hear you properly," said Sam.

"It's this leaf holding my chin. I can't open my mouth properly." As she spoke Sally could smell and taste the sweet smell of custard in the air, then a smell of chocolate oranges. As she wriggled her head from side to side she began to taste the juices of the leaf. Sally stuck out her tongue.

"Emm emm Sam have a bite of these leaves. They are soooperb," whispered Sally. The leaves were multicoloured. On one side it was chocolate covered and inside was cream. On the other side it was orange and so on. Some were black and white tasting of liquorice or strawberry with blackberry on the other side.

"These are the same leaves the gentle people wanted us to eat Sam. Have a taste. This is good nosh bro." Sally bent her head and chewed on the leaves. She had been eating for what seemed like hours but could only have been minutes. They had been ignored by the flies so Sally continued to eat her fill of this new food. After a while she began to feel woozy, her head began to spin, her legs were beginning to tingle and shake, her tiny muscles began jumping around, and her eyes were shining like a torch.

"Oh Sam I do feel ill, like I am going to die," cried Sally.

Sam heard this and began to panic. "Don't die on me Sally. I will never find my way home and what if I do. What will I say to Mum and Dad?" Sam then noticed Sally smiling a funny weird wicked smile.

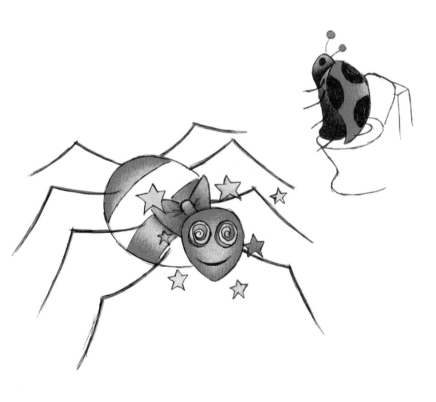

"Hey Sam, what are those sparkling things in front of my eyes, everything is going bluey purple, white and red?"

Sally had begun to hallucinate. The leaves were acting as a drug and would give her super powers.

"Look, check out the ladybird on the toilet," shouted an excited Sally.

"What toilet? Which ladybird?" said a confused Sam, "What is wrong with you Sally?"

"Don't know, but I feel sooperb!"

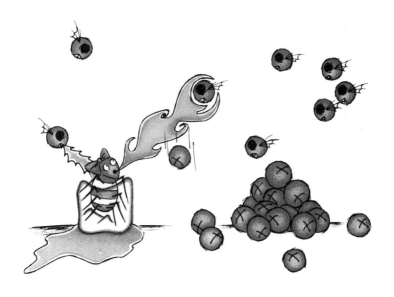

Chapter 6

THE ICE PRISON

Meanwhile, Sally's body was dramatically changing. Her body was changing colour, that is to say, Sally's temperature was rising. Her skin began to glow, pink then red. Sally quickly realised that the ice cube was melting, so too did the flies. They swarmed forward to attack, spraying ice cold vapour onto Sally. Yet, as quickly as they did this, Sally was melting the ice holding her. Her super powers were taking over. As more flies arrived to drive home the attack, Sally found the melting ice allowed her some movement. She drew in a large breath of air and blew out a poisonous gas that drifted above the fighting flies killing thousands. More flies arrived to attack her. The battle raged like this for over an hour. Sally melted the ice as the flies poured more icy vapour over her. Then a signal saw the flies pull back.

Sally stood exhausted watched by creatures and insects who had started to arrive. Some began to believe she could just win, while others thought she was going to lose.

"One more attack and she will be finished," moaned some as they began hurriedly making their way home before the flies attacked them too. Again the flies attacked. At one point she disappeared from view as the flies surrounded her, pouring more icy vapour over her. The ice was now ten times the original thickness and yet Sally continued to melt it. As her body became white hot the ice turned to water and as this happened the flies began to shrivel up with the intense heat generated by Sally.

Suddenly the fighting stopped. The flies were in retreat. The flies were walking or flying away and after about thirty minutes they had disappeared.

It had been a huge battle. Bodies of flies lay everywhere. Pile upon pile of them lay where they had fallen.

Looking around she saw Sam still a prisoner of his ice cube and still tied up. Still radiating intense heat she quickly freed him and the butterfly. With herself now cooling down, both she and Sam hugged each other. At last the flies were beaten. Lots of creatures and insects arrived to praise Sally. A party was started to celebrate. It was while the party was underway that Sally noticed newspaper being read, and on its front page were the headlines:-

Parents want their children home. Feared dead. Drowned.

"Come on Sam we are going home to Mum and Dad." Sally said sorry to everyone,
Our parents need us. We're going home."

And out of the crowd came a huge earthworm.

"I will be going to the human world if you want a lift home, just jump on board."

Sally and Sam climbed on board and the worm started the long journey home. They hung on tight as the worm travelled through a maze of tunnels built by years of travel by other worms. At long last Sally saw light at the mouth of the tunnel. As the worm approached the surface he stopped to look out. Starting again, he slowly pushed his head out into the sunshine. Sam excitedly stood up to get off, but fell over, as the worm moved. Sally grabbed him quickly, pulling him back on board.

"What's happening Sal?"

'I don't know."

The worm began to jerk backwards and forwards, but it was not a jerk more of a stretching. The worm seemed to be getting longer and longer. The front wanted to go out but the rear wanted to stay inside. Sally and Sam were thrown around.
'Go up to the front Sam and see what is happening out there."

"No fear, you go!" said Sam.

"You are shady Sam spider, don't know why I have you for a brother."

"Never mind I'll do it." Sally made her way along the back of the worm, until at last she could look out. The sun blazed into her eyes. At first she thought she was seeing things because of the sun, but she was not.

There in front of her eyes was a crow, with the head of the worm inside its beak, tugging hard to pull the worm out and have a feast.

"Quick Sam, jump down and help to pull the worm back in."

But it was too late. With a final tug the worm with the pair hanging on flew out of the tunnel and high into the air. The crow flew high above the houses and trees, finally settling down on a branch where the nest was. Sitting there were five hungry little crows all with beaks open and begging for food, saliva dribbling down over their feathers at the sight of the delicious worm.

"Me first, Dad," "No me Dad, I never got anything the last time." "Oh! What are those skinny little things?"

"These are spiders, I have not had one since I was about your age."

"Hey Dad, they have got legs, mmm, crunchy, juicy bones."

"Well then, let's see who's first"

Bending down the crow picked up Sally and moved across the nest to drop her into the mouth of his favourite chick. Meanwhile, Sally had become upset at the thought of dying for a second time and had begun to get angry and was getting hotter and hotter.

The crow dropped Sally head first into the chick's mouth. As he bent down to pick up Sam, a horrible scream filled the air, like when a child gets a clout around the ear, or when someone traps a finger in a door, or bites their tongue.

"Oh, ouch, ah, ah, get it out Dad, it is burning my mouth."

The crow rushed round and slapped his chick hard on the back and out flew Sally. She was glowing red-hot. As soon as she landed in

the nest it started to burn, and so too did the crows, jumping around as the nest smouldered and their feathers singed. The smallest chick died almost straight away. The leaves on the tree and its branches were smouldering, with smoke everywhere. Everyone's eyes were filling with smoke. The crows flew off, leaving Sally, Sam and the worm. After a while Sally calmed down and cooled down, the trio decided the only way out was down, and down below them was the house washing line. It was all covered in blankets, jumpers, towels etc.

"We will all jump into the clothes, there we will all be safe," urged Sally, and then jumped.

As they floated down, a gentle breeze came and carried them away from the washing line until thud, they had landed.

"Are we dead?" whispered Sam.

"I doubt it," uttered Sally.

They had landed in the fur of the house cat, Smokey. Smokey had been asleep and woke when they crashed into her. Opening her eyes Smokey spotted a large bee just in front of her and about to land on a flower for a feed. Thinking it was the bee that had woken her up, she gave chase into the flowerbed, pouncing into the flowers looking for the bee. The bee had been hurt and dazed but was also angry.

"What a joker," said the bee, limping across the soil and hiding under the remaining flower heads.

The cat gave up and strolled onto the lawn, preparing to settle down again for a snooze. When wham, the bee had recovered and stung the cat in the bum, and was preparing to dive and sting the cat again, joined by a friend.

"Get off you barmy bees!" yelled Smokey.

"No fear, it was you who hurt me first, you will get what you deserve."

Smokey turned and ran but was cornered with her back against a tree. The bees were high in the air, their tails rasping, loaded with sting ready for poor Smokey. The trio was still clinging to the fur of the cat.

"What if they hit us instead of Smokey?" Cried the worm.

"You're right," thought Sally, "but what can we do?"

Then almost without thinking she began to weave a web around Smokey, who was confused but grateful for the help. Sally had just finished when the bees struck like supersonic jets, they whistled through the air with enough sting to kill Smokey. They spotted the web when it was too late to stop. Their tails flew straight into and out of the other side of the web, only millimetres away from Smokey's terrified face. The bees were now caught in Sally's strong web.

"Hey man, my wings, I cannot move 'em!"

"Me neither."

It was too late, Sally had begun to wrap them up whilst they had been talking.

"Hey this is not right, we have been trapped by a silly baby spider. Come on kid, let us go" urged the bees, now held tightly.

"Look, we will not hurt you, just this crazy cat." They said

Sally could see they were worried, but was going to teach them a lesson.

"I have not eaten for months, I will have you for my dinner tonight, I will just go and get my Mum and Dad, they will be proud of me, capturing two big bees."

"Look kid," said the oldest bee, terrified "what if we promise to bring you food, you know honey, flies the odd moth that way you'll never be hungry again and bees always keep their word."

Sally really was not bothered about all of this, she was happy the bees had learnt a lesson. Smokey was so grateful she carried Sally and Sam into the house

"I will hide you in the bathroom, there is a radiator there and you can live behind the sink."

CHAPTER 7

THE HUMANS

The bathroom was spotless, on one wall was the toilet, a sink and a bath. The most interesting object in the room was spotted high at ceiling level. Clinging to a light directly above the bath was a big juicy wasp fast asleep and unaware that Sally and Sam had just arrived. The bath was full of water and a boy was playing with his toys.

"Just look Sam, proper food , it is ages since we ate a decent meal. We can surprise Mum and Dad, they will be hungry too."

Without waiting, Sally started to climb to get to the wasp before it woke up and flew off. She had to first climb the wall and then walk along the ceiling to where the wasp lay asleep. Carefully lowering herself down to the level of the wasp, she began to quietly and quickly spin a web around the unsuspecting wasp, but with only a couple of threads wrapped around, the wasp woke up. With fear and realising it was going to be eaten, it nervously decided to go to the toilet and dropped a dollop of wasp turd into the bath water, splashing the little boy, who was furious and looking up spotted the wasp above, called his Mum.

'Mum, a lump of wasp turd just missed my head!"

As he said this, Sally, who had been trying hard to trap the wasp lost all her energy and fell into the water.

The little boy spotting Sally fall into the water again yelled loudly to his mum, "there is a tiny spider now in my bath?"

"Well get out and pull the plug. It will go down the plughole," shouted his mum.

Meanwhile Sally was fighting for her life, trying to overcome the waves of water now washing over her and trying to remember how

Dad taught her to swim. Sally was weak from lack of food and could not manage a stroke and was being carried away with the rush of water, unable to beat its suction.

The boy had left the room and his mum had arrived, preparing to clean out the bath after her son. She had not noticed a second spider arrive who was standing on the bath side. Sam could see Sally swirling around below him in the water.

"Kick your legs Sally like Dad taught you!" shouted Sam. But the force of the water was getting stronger. "Hang on Sally, I am coming" shouted Sam as he dived into the soapy swirling water.

The boy's mum stood motionless at the side of the bath. Her mouth had dropped open. She had not moved from the spot for what seemed like ages when suddenly she put down her cleaning cloth and knelt at the bath side.

Maggie, the mum, was amazed by what she could see and hear. Watching the water swirl around she could also see and hear Sally shouting and fighting for her life.

"Get closer Sam, get hold of my hair or my legs if you can."

"I'm trying Sally. It's impossible. We're going to die."

"No Sam! We are not. Just get hold of my hair it will be ok," shouted Sally.

At first Maggie thought it was just voices drifting in from outside. Then she quickly realised it was these two spiders in her bath. She quickly called her husband and son.

"Come here quickly you two. I cannot believe this but there are spiders in the water talking and shouting for help."

"Oh ye and I suppose they are swimming, doing the crawl or breast stroke," laughed her husband.

"No seriously, come here. These two really are talking. Talking English too. Listen!"

Husband and son arrived just before Sally and Sam went down the plughole, screaming. The whole bathroom echoed with their little voices shouting for their Mum and Dad.

Sam had just grabbed Sally when the rush of water forced them both into a mass of human hair, wet and slimy from all the shampoos. It dangled down into the plughole. The inside of the plughole was dark and wet. Sally realised her hair was tangled around the human hair and it was this that stopped their fall.

"Quick Sam get a hold of the hair before we fall," urged Sally.

"I can't Sally. It is too wet and slimy" cried Sam.

Sally was also aware she had broken a leg and so could not climb. It was up to Sam to do it. Sally barked an order.

"Sam! Start tying the human hair into little knots. That way we can start to climb up and out of here. When you get to the top you will have to pull me up."
"Ok," shouted Sam.

And off he started, tying the human hair into knots. Sam worked slowly, knot after knot he climbed but each time he seemed to get higher he slid back down.

"What are you doing Sam? I can't hold on much longer," cried Sally.

"I cannot do it, Sally. Each time I climb I slide back down. The slimy hair makes it impossible to keep my grip."

Now Maggie had heard all this and decided to help them.

"Right you two," she said to her husband and son "find some string, anything we can push through these holes in the plug or go get your tools and take the plughole off. We must save these spider children."

"But they are not humans so why should we" said her husband.

"Because they have a right to live, like anything else that lives. You can hear them talk like I can."

"Emm I get it. If they are our spiders we could get rich. Instant celebrities, the first spiders to talk living with us. You are so clever Maggie."

"Me clever! We are not going to do any of that. We are going to save these children. Ok!"

Meanwhile Sally had an idea. You see, she could not spin a web or climb the hair because it was all wet but if she could dry it, then they would get a chance to climb out. But how? How do you dry anything that is wet through?

"How do we dry this hair Sam so we can climb out," cried a tired Sally.

Almost at once, just like turning the lounge lights on, Sam had an idea. Looking across at Sally, who by now was looking ill and still hanging on tightly to the human hair. Sam knew he had to act fast or his sister and he would fall into the water below and possibly drown.

"Sally," shouted Sam as he struggled to free a leg.   "I have got something for you."

As Sally turned her head to look at Sam he gave her a hard kick.

"Ouch!   Sam! I will kill you, that really hurt you shady spider" screamed Sally, who became so angry she began to get hot and hotter until she was glowing. Sam hid behind the wet slimy hair to shield him from Sally's heat. Sally became so hot the hair in the plughole had dried, some of it starting to burn.   At that very moment the plastic plughole just went POP, like a balloon bursting. Out onto the bathroom floor fell Sally and Sam. The whole thing made Sally cool down and she and Sam hugged each other.

"We are free Sam. Let's find Mum and Dad. Oh hold on a second Sam. I owe you a hard kick after doing that to me."

"No Sally. You don't, I knew I had to make you angry so you would get hot and the hair would dry. But you got so angry you melted the plastic plughole."

"You are so clever Sam Spider. A bit daft and stupid at times, but clever my bro."

The pair had been so excited chatting they had not become aware of three pairs of human eyes peering at them. Sally first spotted the problem and instinctively grabbed Sam.

"Over there Sam, into this crack in the floor boards." As they ran it became obvious Sally was in a lot of pain from her broken leg.

"You run Sam. Save yourself. Run for the crack in the floor."

"No Sally come on, I will carry you." Sam tried but could not pick her up. Grabbing one of Sally's legs he began dragging her along the floor. As they struggled they noticed a wall of towels had been placed over their hiding place.

"Back Sam. Run the other way, go on save yourself, save yourself bro."

"No. You are coming with me sis" screamed Sam.

Then the human voice of Maggie sounded, quietly almost in a whisper she said "Little spiders we can hear you talking, every word. We do not want to hurt you. We want to help you. Just stop running away and talk to us. We are sorry. We did not realise spiders had feelings and could talk. We always thought you were like the flowers or grass that we cut down and throw away. Not important but you are important."

"But we are not flowers or grass. We are spiders with Mums and Dads. We've uncles and aunts just like you" shouted Sally.

Sally stopped and listened. She was amazed she was communicating with humans. It was at that time Maggie said "How can we hear you and how are you talking to us?"

"I am not sure," said Sally. "It may be to do with something I have eaten but just now it doesn't matter."

"Come here get onto my finger" said Maggie.

"I can't move. MY leg is broken. It will be a couple of days before it fixes itself," said Sally.

Looking closer Maggie could see a leg dangling, not really a part of Sally.

"Look," said Maggie. "You can help your sister by pulling her gently onto this cloth. Then I will be able to lift you both off the floor and onto our kitchen table downstairs. There you will be safe and we can talk properly."

Within five minutes the pair were sitting downstairs chatting with Maggie's family. Then Sally heard a scream. It was her Mum.

"Hold on Sally, I am coming" shouted her Mum.

This was funny for Sally. You see, she could hear Mum and

Maggie but neither Mum nor Maggie could see or hear each other. As Sally watched Mum climbing up to save her, Sally and Sam started to giggle, a sort of 'safe' giggle and shouted to their Mum.

"Stay there Mum. We will come and get you. These humans are gentle. We are safe here."

Sally quickly explained to Maggie what was happening. Maggie looked down and could see two spiders climbing upwards. Cupping her giant hands she scooped up Mum and Dad and placed them on the table next to Sally and Sam.

The children excitedly told their parents the whole adventure, finishing with Maggie and her family.

Maggie began to realise how important it was for Sally's parents to be back with their children. Maggie's family, plus their cat, fell in love with Sally and Sam and together they became one big happy family.

THE END